AF432056

Dedication

For all my loved now dead ones,
Especially Daddy, Pauline, Jay and Joy
Mom Wood, Dad Wood,
and Pastor Greaves and Sister Greaves.

This was a hard season.
All I bring you are these few humble seeds,
Hoping my feminist machinations can
Bring good fruit.

Acknowledgements

I thank Jah for guidance and for friends. I could not have done this without Cherrylene Young and Ife Harris. They were my formal CAFRA (Caribbean Association For Feminist Research and Action) committee that forced me to collate these poems. Cherrylene typed it, Ife gave shots of confidence from the sidelines, being herself a dub poet, and they both offered the supportive energy to get it off to the Frank Collymore Literary Endowment Awards where I/we won second prize to Kamau Brathwaite! We seek guidance as we launch it out as an ever-returning gift for International Women's Days and other celebrations of peacefulness.

Published by:
MARGARET D. GILL

Paperback Edition
ISBN: 978-976-96713-1-7

Cover Photographer: Margaret D. Gill
Portrait Photographer: Gordon Stewart
Design & Formatting: Grafixx 2 Inc.

Preface

Some have wondered bout the name I give this book, Machinations of a Feminist. One even offered the comment in an email: "i don't like this title. nvr have, from the moment I hear it. is too MACHINERY for the kind of lyrics you put down in the collection. nor are you and your ideas Machiavellian." I must admit it was a little daunting that this comment came from my friend, mentor and Ancestor Poet, Kamau Brathwaite; however, it was not daunting enough to make me change my title! This book has a secret intent which you shall discover upon reading, and so its name begins that journey of the Anancy spider woman.

Kamau struck a nerve that triggered the defense I subsequently use as this preface (his suggestion):

"By the way, Kamau, a Feminist, like a Christ-ian is never intentionally machiavillain, and so generally cannot practice machinations. I am making a deliberate effort to be both mechanic and showing people the lyrics I fixing- like if I tek my car ta ah machiavillain an cahn afford the parts nor the labour that he fixup. I am, in other words, making form and function brek friendship. Is like frigging spiders for twice de increase, as old Barbados used to say.

When the readers them done watch the lyrics that they buy, another help gone forth ta lend that hand them never know that them extend. And who ta hold it but another weeping one. Here I meaning how this book is partly a fund-raiser for projects for a CAFRA Barbados violence against the girl-child and HIV/AIDS.

Listen, consider how many anti-Feminists who think that Feminism is about Machiavellianism, and dey using form and function prose-respectability to say we machinating. And dey is get way wid it too! Same thing some doing wid Christ-ians. But as I say in "That Man", "ya have ta watch ya back, boy."

I may be trying to be ah -ian, but I ain't anti-Feminist. Plus, I glad somebody ask me to bear That Man and all those Machinations of a Feminist, which tittle, jot and title, Kamau, I keeping.

An as regards your problem, Kamau, with my words "ubiquitous chemistry" in one poem, I beg to disappoint, I also keeping that! "It sound too prosey"! Does not exist anywhere in prose, nowhere! Not in no prose, nowhere in no prose does it allow chemistry to be "ubiqutous". None! I keeping that. Pablo Neruda did not surrender "lugubrious blue." I will defend this yet unfinished spider woman voice in all humility.

Kamau responded, "gotcha on the 'ubiquitous chemistry.'"

Margaret D. Gill
Cave Hill
2008-04-30

TABLE OF CONTENTS

Who Knows

LOVE LIES SLEEPING

On windy sunday afternoons,
dry season,
windblown scraps
find refuge at a town-drunk' s back.

Lettuce leaves rot passively
beside her outstretched
sleeping arm,
while children's sunday voices chime
from the eves of bright cathedrals.

Oh, let her sleep!
Oh, let her sleep!

She dreams of woodoves
and the ground-dove's
murmurous coo.

QUE

*(Everything has its own signature frequency. What if the rabbit's fear
causes its heart to beat at the same frequency as the planet's?)*

I am as enraged as
the rabbit's trembling heart,
as cunning as
the fox's cunning Q,
but dey tell me be dove and love,
and please to wait
the process through.

So loving them I try,
compose my crippled angst,
my sorry self and my
volcanic blues.
I try to cramp inside the inside of my pain -
but dis en mekking nah sense, fah true!

Don't hold me back
I going through;
I tekking up the courage of my broken heart, its
que.
And see me? I getting outta hey!
Is true!

TREK TO 'COW PASTOR'

(For Beverley and Kamau Brathwaite)

("A king is somebody who if his shoes want polishing he don't ask his servants; he is polish them himself." as explained by Khary Gill, when he was a child of about 7 years old. He was explaining his name which means Kingly One.)

I descend the track to Cow Pastor,
Rough and uncouth as my heart,
Praying that the king
Would extend his scepter to me
And that I would not otherwise die;
And that the queen
Would enfold me
In her singularly righteous embrace.
She embraces me and
The day grows strangely warm.

The smell of gold cane
In the morning,
Loosed now by one man and machine
Is my uncertain context.
So too the wound
That is my heart
When they return,

As always they must return
To uncomely planets
Where I cannot follow like the lost sheep
That I am.

Oh, Wait!
Oh, do not leave me here
Where corbeaux gather on the line
Above our lives,
Where there is sure knowledge
That your leave without play,
Without pay,
Has finally played out
And you must leave us here.

> But looka how we stay?
> Standing in the king's gate,
> Kin to the oppressed,
> Waiting for winter to end?

WHO SAYS WHITE MEN.

*(In thankfulness for the USIS labour fellowship that allowed me the
education from staying at all the best hotels across seven states from
Washington DC to Alaska.)*

Who says White Men?
Do they mean Phillip, or Shane or Jesse?
They have my affection.

Who says White Men?
Is it Rob they talking bout?
Or is it Ian?

Do they mean Lawrence
Who oftentimes distresses me,
But who, somehow, I liked?
Who says White Men?

Who says White Men?
Could they be talking about Pete?
Pete who loves his sons
And taps them round the head
When they behaving rude?
Could they possibly mean Pete?

What about Allan?
Is it Allan they talking bout
When they say
White Men, White Men?

The Maitre D,
Forgetting he was on "Millionaire Mile" -
Or possibly remembering-
Asked, "Can I help you?"
Not, "The number of your party?" No,
Not, "Welcome" .
Not even merely "Morning Ma'am" but
"Can I help you?"

Does he expect me to call
For a pound of pig trotters?
Or perhaps a bushel of salt?
Or is he possibly one of the crew
Of White Men, White Men?

What could I do, Charles,
What would you do?
I'm sure I heard him say,
"White Men White Men."
Richard, didn't you hear him say
White men?

LETTER TO MY DEAD SISTER

(For Pauline)

I confess myself
a little envious.
Not of your absences,
etched with that impartial
chisel, death, on the
not – nearly granite materials
of my broken heart;

Not of your silent voices
present now only in the
permanent recesses of
my echoing ear drums,
But envious of your descent
into the heart of things.

Assuredly, your descent
into the heart of things
is for the redemption of loving.

Listen, under the clank and clamour
of each day's jousts, I know,
love's word is scarcely ever heard.

Listen, I am tired of pretending
that I do not miss you. That is all.
For I do. I do.

ALTERNATIVE FEMINISM

Sleeping Beauty's problem
Was not that she was
Waiting for the man.
After all, is not she send
And call he?

It was
her
sleeping
till he
come.

SUCCEED!

(For Cuba 12-10-1995 and to Hugo Chavez)

Succeed! For you hold
our banner of Most
Favoured Nation status.
Succeed! For resistance
is a place where we must kneel
only in honour of liberation
and not as concession to need.

Succeed!

And the children will come leaping
Over this newest challenge
That threatens to fail you.
Succeed! Succeed! Succeed!

HEARTLAND

I was born a with a whole
In my heart
Through which falls
Fairly ordinary things:

> Trees, rhinestone earrings,
> Grass pearls, trilldren,
> 2 odd epaulets of my son
> Khary's
> And the simply simple
> ridiculous laughter
> Of a bobolee.

Whole hurricanes and a hibiscus
Fall there;
One man and his two-bit stupidity;
A friend who did not understand bi-polar crisis
And so, she left me;

3 projects,
1 crisis centre,
2 essays and a calypsonian
Who sings the folly
That for boys to excel
Girls must not be.

Like if excellent get limit!
And girls belong to secondly!

You! Whole dry spells and
A bougainvillea fall there.

I am not ah idiot, or mad, or stupidee.
I just have a whole in my heart
For all humanity[1]

---

1   The punctuation to placed after humanity is the sign
epsilon – the sideways 8 – rather than a question mark. The
idea is to turn the "y" into the the Spanish word for "and"
and make the humanity become humanity and all. I do not
know how to get that sign on my computer.

ANTIQUES AT LOWER GREEN

(For Omo and Laura, Kently and Lillette)

Love to see them old lovers,
When each other's flesh has become sacred
Through the years of touching;

When love has rooted
In the bone,
The blood's limit,
To the heart's last wall.

Love to see them old lovers
When silences have grown warm
With shared vocabularies,
With quiet permissions,
With appreciation.

I see the care
In their protective gestures,
Their willingness to wait,
To gather in,
To acknowledge;

How every act
Is a love occasion,

An act to commit affection;
Bearing fragrances of past seductions,
So that even the bad times
With you are sweet.

Moreover,
I see the grace of love gone antique,
And all I can wish is

    That you become old lovers.

RECIPE: THE SORREL

Not liking bullies
or the way how, once She'd called
a person, how this
world just gang up on her back,
seeking to hold her back,
backing her into every little corner
crack and crevice, God just took
God's mixing spoon,
and just like how
you'd part that sorrel drink
to mix the sugar in,
displacing liquid to the left
and to the right,
just for a second, as
you'd see a slice of saucepan bottom
rise up like a silver pathway
and the scent of spices-
clove, the bayleaf, cinnamon,
a dash of Agostura-
rise up through the dark red waves,
God part that sea,
and watch how woman walk cross!

Alternatives

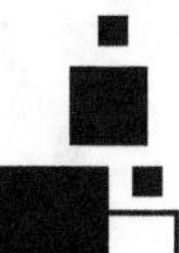

ON SEEING

*(written at Enterprise Beach, Oistins, which early morning Barbadians
might lose to development.)*

This morning the arch angel Gabriel
Stood quietly by the orange lifeguard tower.
The curve of his lower back
Was the same pain as mine
And I could in the distance hear
Melodic cackling
Of the seraphim.

But he was steady as the blue.

Behind him was this old Raleigh black bicycle,
his;
His clothes respectfully resting near
That sheltered corner where
I, by habit, store my poems

Good morning, I said.
Is it going to rain and wreck my work?
"No", he replied, "except the clouds
Are in that southwest corner of the sky."

I note the grace in his deep eyes,
His dreadlocked care,
(his hair like mine)
his awesome kindliness.

Was like the time I turned
The corner by the hardware store,
And suddenly, block upon block
Was harmonic, was celestial;

And that group of Y De Lima Clerks
In their blue tee shirts
Was a contingent of the heavenly host.
And when I told them so
They laughed and swore
That they were only Y De Lima Clerks.

Except that I could swear,
By the effulgence of the blue,
The way the light hosannahed down the valley
of that street,
And their embarrassed laughter,
I'd happened on the truth.

HURRICAN IVAN II

(For Preston)

If I could bend the light
transform its possibilities
fix its eternity in time
release its ubiquitous chemistry
its charity and clarity of thought;

if I could get its permission
to glow, to conform, to expand
and educate;

> Could I present you with
> the Ivan Eye of judgement
> and thus break your heart,
> I would just shelter you with
> photographs
> and thus I'd share such loving

Jah, you'd be amazed!

A'WRITE THEN

(More sea...)

I hope you know how I feel bout you sea.
When I see you my heart
Does fall down pon its scarlet knee.
If I could faint from loving
It would only be
With you sea, sea, sea, sea!

Sea, I hoping you en hear
Wha dem tell me -
That there will be no sea
In the new eternity.
If dat is true I gine down pon
My other knee
And wrestle God to come up with
A new plan D,
Sight!

If dey going be no sea
In the new eternity
Where we gun bathe?
Which part I gun find a wave,
To walk in?
How people gun exercise

Pon de beach if dum en got nah sea!

How come dah gun got a new Heaven
And a new Earth, but
Nah new sea?

I really don't understand this Lord. Unless,
Unless You really mean
dum en gun got
Neffing separating people?

"A'write den!"

PRESTON

I wear you like a redolent bouquet

And am surprised that people do not know.

Except that the men say,

I smell like pheromones.

DISAVOWAL

(For Amy)

There is the sea
In this poem.
It will come roaring down
The cantilever of this shy metre.
It will crash through the once resilient
Break water of my heart.

Here, the sea avows its imagery of salt
It disperses round globulets
Of verse violently,
Reeking, all the same,
Of green forgiveness.

It will cling and touch like velvet.
It will cling, somehow, like moss.
About this encroaching tenderness
I can do nothing, I tell you,
Nothing!

There is the sea in this poem
And its sound is wide,
Impartial,
Bounteous as the sea.

THAT MAN

I could just smell him there,
The blood, the stink of his perspiration,
And the urine! Nobody ever talks about the
urine,
Or the flies,
But these too were there.

I could almost still hear the echoes of his
anguish,
Of his fear.
His impossibly kind words
Fretting the afternoon air.

Christ! What did he expect?
Those boys were into hard ball.
They did not care for anything
Except being right

And seeing the Synagogue takings swell.

And the others?
Well, a better set of sheep,
And cowards,
And down-right worthless carrion
I cannot imagine.

I know! I know.
You go tell me bout he mother
And he friends,
Even that one that all Jerusalem had
Till she turn salvation and now making saint.

So how come they never say nothing?
'Ya have ta watch ya back, boy.'
'Partner, you really sure bout this thing?'
Anything, just to turn he back.

And we en even going to start pon he father!

All I know is,
look how all down the years now
I will have to bear that man.
Christ! And nobody nevah asked me nutten!

NAMELESS DREAD: A SONNET

'but for the grace....'

Faster than we can count you multiply,
or so it seems, as each street casts anew
some ship wrecked soul on our reluctant view
and intersects our need to hurry by,
setting our faces from you, as we try
To mute the censure and reclaim our due-
Our city sanitized; no sign of you
To wreck the vision, or refute the lie.

But with your layers of grime and of neglect,
You stand between ambition and the truth.
A testimony to our own decline
Of spirit; witness, as we stand aloof
Of a deep fear we struggle to reject:
That fate alone divides our lot from thine.

WORDSONG OF MORNING[2]

I like the taste or morning
Smell of smoky dark
Interiors of chattel houses

Liking the taste of morning
With its lives and lines of laundry
Wet slapping lines of skirt tails, shirts,
Drying modest undergarments.

This morning word-song
Is the whistled chant
Of tender sparrows
Black birds making words
With government children.
They with their loud contrary livity
Give thanks for morning.

---

2 As this poem proceeds hold in your mind a small east Indian woman being beaten outside my parents working-class home on a quiet Sunday afternoon when I was eleven, and a young white woman crying in the late night as her partner drags her along the road holding her arm through his car window. I hear her through my window in my house in a Barbadian height and terrace and I am fifty three.

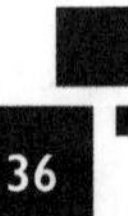

Give thanks for morning
And the men who make it
Clean

They come with faces set
Against the hills of sour refuse

Thanks, give thanks! For
These men work to raze
The hills of refuse

Thanks, give thanks! They
Leave behind a clean
Green smell of lemon balm
And the stench of sacred sweat, give thanks!

Eh ehhh! Give thanks I say
Give thanks!
For good news neighbours:
My long gone brother
Who returns:

He is grating cassava with our mother
He is helping Mama sort fish

Give thanks I say, give thanks!

HURRICANE IVAN I

The red one of death
Comes striding over the clouds
And he is calling my name,
But he will call in vain.

He will call, but will not hear I speak,
For Jah is holding I,
Withholding I.

Jah will take back I name, Or
Jah will let one call it.

Regardless,
Morning is, without a doubt,
coming, coming

THE JUSTIFIABLE LAMENT

I know the Revolution was postponed.
We had wanted to consolidate
Unsteady kingdoms
On our indisputable way to upwards,
In order, and I remember well, that we
Could wheel and better come again;
To face walled streets and
Unassailable stone eyes.

But when did you decide
I did not need to see you?

I did agree,
And again, remember well,
That kamakazie strategies,
And all that talk of God
Were just passé

In the grand ordinary scheme of things
Negotiation is appropriate and
Just plain right.

But recall for me,
We had consulted on all this vast

Oblivion of loving?
And I had said what?
I had said what, exactly?

In my naivety, perhaps,
Perhaps infantile insecurity,
It just seemed fixed-
Communion.
Our keen attentiveness to us and
To reciprocal tenderness:
This faith.

I paused to draw necessary breath
And suddenly,
Your customary scent
is wanting in my atmosphere.

So.
Now I resort to the gathering
Of assumptions.

To the forging of clinical
Indivisible codes
That would restore my roots,

Seeking, as I do, to scale
No less than the roof

Of this blasted world.
No less than the roof of this blasted world.

Look how again
Is me alone and the moon out there...

FOR RENE

Maybe the body's husk
Is but a chrysalis we weave
and wrap to warm
our naked spirit, that at some
point undresses
and we burn into the depths
as stars.

Maybe our varied and awesome beauty
Is but grass;
Is harvested some importunate
And utterly impetuous day,
Only to scatter the seeds
Of our bright souls
Into the welcoming and
Ever lasting nebulae!

MY SECOND CALYPSO

(No weapons of mass destruction...)

This war is Bush fault
Not Bin Laden's.
But Bin Laden is also to blame.
And all ah we silent complicit,
And guilty as rhahn gate[3]!

---

3 A Barbadian/Bajan euphemism for another Bajan curse word which as we say shall remain nameless.

MISUNDERSTANDING

Land calls to the sea:
Come wid it. Come!
Sea comes and comes again.

> Hysterical ferocity
> Phallic abandon
> ment

INTEGRITY OF FLESH

(For Pauline and for Jane who cried)

Before they bury me
will anybody be there
to brush the moth out of my hair,
because my casket is open
and they left me there
lying in this third world third rate
funeral home
no aircondition
and the windows open
where the moths come in?
Before they bury me
Will anybody be there?

Before they bury me
will anybody be there
who will cover my head
and dress me so my flesh
will remember who I
was?

You see, the chemo took
my crowing glory.
Will anybody be there

to get the exact Afro wig
to arrange my accustomed little vanities
before they bury me?
Will anybody be there?

Will anybody touch my cold hands
or look on me longingly?
Will the neighbours come?
Will anybody at work comfort
my smallest sister and the others,
and my son especially
who I see there?
Will the earth be gentle?

YOU

(For Pauline)

If I should encounter
In the clean morning
Before they bury the dead,
Unfolding their long litany of loved ones,
Each carefully pinpointed
Like the keen points of the diamond that we are
To the dead and all-

> Margaret, labourer at
> the university
> Mother of khary,
> smallest sister
> Of the beloved
> deceased,
> And the daughter, and
> so on-

If on this sort of morning,
With a chill rain coming
Off the Atlantic
Sudden and quarrelsome,
That rushes me to close windows,
Hence, to the delight

Of the rain exclaiming
Through the sun exclaiming!

                    Incandescent morning,
                    morning of mosaic
                    woodoves[4]
                    wildflower morning of
                    vermillion boats
                    of fishermen
                    ascending the bridge
                    of heaven,
                    braving the subdued
                    growl
                    of taciturn seawater;

If I should think of you
On just this sort of morning,
Then it would become clear
Why all I could see, sister, sister,
When they buried you from me,
Were so many, many yellow butterflies.

---

4 For performance of this poem I insert the sound here that
the woodove makes. Barbadians say the doves sing: "mo-ses
-speak -God's- word.

Margaret D. Gill taught, variously, literature, written english, Caribbean civilization studies and critical writing for over two decades as adjunct staff at the Cave Hill Campus of the University of the West Indies. She has been published in several anthologies, including the original BIM Magazine and The Oxford Book of Caribbean Verse (2005). She was First Prize winner of the Inaugural Frank Collymore Literary Endowment Award (1998), and in 2008 was one of nine international writers of the IWW. Visiting writers made media appearances, shared their work and interacted with students and staff at several universities in Hong kong and China.